THOMAS JEFFERSON

ENCYCLOPEDIA of PRESIDENTS

Thomas Jefferson

Third President of the United States

By Jim Hargrove

CHILDRENS PRESS ®

CHICAGO

**Independence Hall in Philadelphia, Pennsylvania,
where the Declaration of Independence was signed**

Library of Congress Cataloging-in-Publication Data

Hargrove, Jim.
　　Thomas Jefferson.

　　(Encyclopedia of presidents)
　　Includes index.
　　Summary: Traces the life of the tall red-headed
Virginian, from his early education and involvement in
the American Revolution to his activities as the
nation's third president and last years at Monticello.
　　1.　Jefferson, Thomas, 1743-1826—Juvenile literature.
2.　Presidents—United States—Biography—Juvenile
literature.　[1.　Jefferson, Thomas, 1743-1826.
2.　Presidents]　I.　Title.　II.　Series.
E332.79.H37　1986　　973.4′6′0924　[B]　[92]　86-9658
ISBN 0-516-01385-8

Picture Acknowledgments

The Bettmann Archive—5, 11 (2 pictures), 14,
16, 26, 32 (2 pictures), 39 (left), 51, 53, 56, 57,
68, 72, 75, 78, 82, 83, 84, 85, 86, 87, 89
H. Armstrong Roberts—4, 6, 28 (bottom), 29
(2 pictures), 39 (right), 40, 42, 45, 46, 48, 52,
80
Historical Pictures Service—10, 17, 24, 25, 62,
66, 69, 73
Library of Congress—8, 12, 13, 18, 23, 30, 31,
34, 36, 37, 38, 41, 54, 65, 67, 74 (top), 79, 88
© Nawrocki Stock Photo—55, 60 (2 pictures), 61
(3 pictures)
North Wind Picture Archives—15, 19, 28 (top),
43, 58, 74 (2 center pictures), 76 (2 pictures), 77
(2 pictures)
Virginia Historical Society—20, 50
U.S. Bureau of Printing and Engraving—2

Cover design and illustration by
Steven Gaston Dobson

The Jefferson Memorial in Washington, D.C.

Table of Contents

The battle at Concord bridge, Massachusetts, began the American
Revolution. Poet Ralph Waldo Emerson later wrote that these
"embattled farmers . . . fired the shot heard round the world."

Chapter 1

The Words Read
'Round the World

In colonial America, the roads from central Virginia to Philadelphia were hardly roads at all. Sometimes the route was marked by trampled-down weeds and grass, often by dirt and mud. For travelers, it was impossible to hurry and easy to get lost.

In May of 1776, a young lawyer from Virginia named Thomas Jefferson needed to get to Philadelphia quickly. He was returning to the meeting of the Second Continental Congress. At that historic gathering, delegates from all thirteen colonies were discussing the grave problems that stood between the American colonists and their British rulers.

As Thomas Jefferson rode northward in his horse-drawn carriage, American colonists were already fighting British soldiers. More than a year earlier, American Minutemen and British redcoats had met in the first battles of the revolutionary war in Massachusetts.

Now, in 1776, an American army under Benedict Arnold was attacking British troops in Canada. In the South, a British army attacked the port city of Norfolk, Virginia, and soon destroyed it. The colony of Virginia, Jefferson's home, was already fighting an undeclared war with Britain.

In September 1774, representatives from twelve of the thirteen American colonies had met in Philadelphia for the First Continental Congress. In May of the following year, the Second Continental Congress began in the same city. Thomas Jefferson, at the age of thirty-two, had been its youngest delegate. At both meetings, the Americans discussed the problems that seemed to be leading them directly into a war. Some of the delegates felt that a battle for independence was the only answer. But others believed that the problems could somehow be solved peacefully.

As he continued on his difficult journey toward Philadelphia, Thomas Jefferson knew that America's war for independence had already begun. He and the other delegates to the Congress faced a difficult task. They had to decide if the scattered fighting that was going on now should become an official war for independence. And if it did, they had to explain to other Americans and to the world why a war was the only answer.

Jefferson had left the Second Continental Congress shortly after Christmas in 1775. Sickness had kept him at his home in Virginia. While he was gone, the North Carolina delegates to the Congress had already been instructed to vote for independence. Delegates from the other colonies would also have to decide how to vote.

Jefferson's house at 702 Market Street in Philadelphia

Thomas Jefferson finally arrived in Philadelphia on May 14, 1776, one week after he had left his home in Virginia. He looked for a place to live while he attended the meetings, and rented an apartment on the second floor of a three-story brick building on Market Street. Less than a month later, he would begin to write the Declaration of Independence in the front parlor of that apartment.

Above: Jefferson's portable liquor cabinet
Right: Jefferson's magnifying glass

Before that, however, he joined the other delegates at the Continental Congress. They liked the thin, almost skinny, Virginian. He was a man of many different talents. He knew several foreign languages, including Latin and Greek. He was an expert mathematician who could calculate when eclipses of the moon and sun would occur. He could design buildings, perform medical operations like an experienced surgeon, survey land, and play the violin. And despite his thinness, he was strong enough to tame a wild horse and chop wood like a lumberjack. Most important of all, he was known to be a superb writer.

One of the few things Jefferson was *not* noted for was his speaking ability. He was shy and seldom spoke out in public. While other delegates at the Congress made long, flowery speeches, Thomas Jefferson just listened.

Richard Henry Lee of Virginia, Jefferson's fellow delegate to the Continental Congress, who urged the Congress to vote for American independence

"During the whole time I sat with him in Congress," said delegate and future U.S. president John Adams, "I never heard him utter three sentences together." But some of the other delegates more than made up for Jefferson's silence. For weeks, their arguments raged. Some wanted independence immediately, others gradually. A few delegates even felt that those who wanted independence should be put in British jails.

The arguments came to a head on Friday, June 7, 1776. On that day, another delegate from Virginia, Richard Henry Lee, rose and asked the Congress to vote on the question of American independence. "Resolved," he began, "that these united colonies are, and of right ought to be, free and independent states. . . ."

The Declaration Committee. Left to right: Thomas Jefferson, Roger Sherman, Benjamin Franklin, Robert Livingston, and John Adams

For several days, the delegates argued whether to vote for or against Lee's resolution. Finally, it was agreed to delay more arguments until July 1. In the meantime, however, a committee was elected to write a Declaration of Independence. Knowing that Jefferson would not rise and speak for himself, John Adams worked tirelessly to get the other delegates to choose the quiet Virginian. Because of Adams's hard work, Thomas Jefferson received the most votes and became the chairman of the committee. The other four members were Adams, Benjamin Franklin, Roger Sherman, and Robert Livingston.

Jefferson was already known throughout the colonies as a fine writer on political questions. So the other members of the committee asked him to write a first draft of the Declaration.

**Jefferson put many hours and much serious thought
into his draft of the Declaration of Independence.**

Jefferson began his work in the parlor of his apartment
on Market Street. For several days, he worked long hours
at a desk, writing the immortal words with pen and ink.
Years later, he wrote that his words were not meant to be
original or creative, but "to be an expression of the
American mind." He used words and phrases that other
American patriots, and even European philosophers, had
used before, so that all could recognize the plain truth of
his statements.

"We hold these truths to be self-evident," he began his
second sentence, "that all men are created equal. . . ." He

Jefferson's rough draft of the Declaration shows how
carefully he searched for the proper wording.

filled his famous document with descriptions of the rights
of people and the many faults of the British king and his
government in America. He concluded by saying that the
people of the "United States of America" declare themselves free of British rule. "And for the support of this
declaration, we mutually pledge to each other our lives,
our fortunes, and our sacred honor."

The young lawyer from Virginia finished the first draft
of the Declaration of Independence in just a few days.
When he showed it to the other four members of the committee, they must have been impressed. John Adams made

Thomas Jefferson, thirty-three years old, reads his draft of the Declaration of Independence to Benjamin Franklin to get his opinion.

only two minor changes, Benjamin Franklin five. Jefferson himself decided that sixteen corrections were needed and added them to a second draft.

On June 28, the five-man committee handed over Jefferson's document to the entire Continental Congress. But the delegates decided not to discuss it until they debated Richard Henry Lee's resolution for independence on July 1. When that day arrived, delegates from all the colonies except South Carolina, Delaware, Pennsylvania, and New York clearly voted for independence.

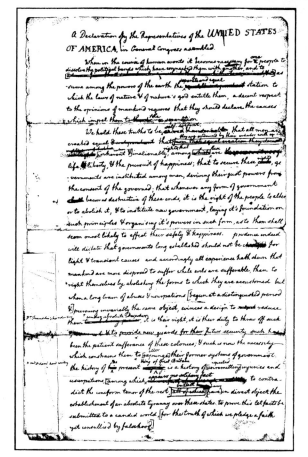
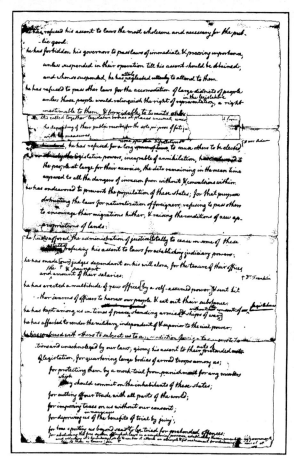

Jefferson's first draft of the Declaration of Independence

As the debates raged on, Jefferson did a most curious thing. Using a thermometer, he began making detailed records of the temperature around the Continental Congress. By the time he would leave the Congress in August, he was recording the temperature, barometric pressure, and wind direction and speed several times each day. He kept making such records for the rest of his long life.

On the following day, July 2, with the delegates from New York not voting and Jefferson still recording the temperature, the Congress voted in favor of independence. The debate then turned to the wording of Jefferson's Declaration of Independence.

The signing of the Declaration of Independence on July 4, 1776

The great debate over Jefferson's words roared throughout the Continental Congress for three days. Some of his harsh criticism against the British king, and especially the British people, was softened. Because some delegates objected, Jefferson's words demanding that no more slaves be brought to America were cut. Rather than join in on the noisy debate, Jefferson quietly listened, and recorded the temperature.

On July 4, 1776, the day the debate finally ended, Jefferson bought an expensive thermometer to replace the less accurate one he had been using. Late in the day, the delegates rose one by one to sign the fateful document. The event marked the end of British rule in the thirteen colonies, the birth of the United States of America, and the beginning of the end of worldwide colonialism. At that historic time, Jefferson noted that the temperature was 73½ degrees.

In Congress, July 4, 1776

The unanimous Declaration of the thirteen united States of America,

The Declaration of Independence in its final form, with signatures

The grounds of the Shadwell estate near Charlottesville, Virginia

Chapter 2

Growing Up in Colonial Virginia

The man who became the third president of the United States was born on April 13, 1743. Because people in the eighteenth century used a slightly different calendar than the one we use today, the date was recorded as April 2. His parents, Peter and Jane Randolph Jefferson, lived in central Virginia. Their home, a large wooden house on a farm they called Shadwell, was about five miles east of the town of Charlottesville.

Thomas Jefferson's home was not quite in the undeveloped Virginia frontier, but settlers were sparse. From Shadwell, the faint image of the Blue Ridge Mountains could be seen to the west. To the south, the land sloped downward to the River Anna. Running near Shadwell was Three Notch'd Road, a major route for travelers moving east or west.

Three Notch'd Road brought many interesting guests to Shadwell. Pioneers, traders, soldiers, and Indians stopped by the Jeffersons' home during their journeys. And Peter Jefferson often found the time to make the guests feel welcome.

Thomas's father was a self-educated man who had served as a sheriff, a justice of the peace, a judge, and a lieutenant in the militia. He was also a rugged outdoorsman, known for his strength and his ability to survey land. Peter Jefferson had married Jane Randolph in October of 1739, when he was thirty-one and she was nineteen. The Randolphs were one of the wealthiest families in Virginia, but beyond that, hardly anything is known of Jane. In all of his many writings, Thomas Jefferson had very little to say about his mother. It has been said that less is known about Jane Jefferson than about the mother of any other famous American.

The Randolph family had a great influence on Thomas Jefferson when he was a young boy. In 1745, William Randolph, a cousin of Jane, died at the age of thirty-three. In his large home in Tuckahoe, Virginia, he left behind a family that included three daughters and a son. A request he made in his will was extremely unusual:

"Whereas I have appointed by my will that my Dear only son Thomas Mann Randolph should have a private education given him at Tuckahoe, my will is that my Dear and loving friend Mr. Peter Jefferson do move down with his family to my Tuckahoe house and remain there till my son comes of age with whom my dear son and his sisters shall live."

A tobacco plantation in the South

Peter and Jane Jefferson agreed to follow the strange request. The fifty-mile trip from Shadwell to Tuckahoe was Thomas Jefferson's earliest memory. He was barely two years old at the time. Tuckahoe was a large plantation, a kind of farm where many different crops were grown and black slaves did much of the farming work.

The plantation system was widespread in the southern U.S. from colonial days until the Civil War. Most people who owned large amounts of land in the South also owned slaves to help work the land. Throughout the South, slaves were used to plant and harvest huge crops of cotton and tobacco. Peter Jefferson had had a few slaves at his small Shadwell plantation, but William Randolph owned more at his much larger plantation. And even though he realized that it was morally wrong, Thomas Jefferson owned slaves throughout his adult life. Slavery was a part of the economic system of the South, and few people, not even Thomas Jefferson, were able to rise above it.

The old mill at Shadwell

When he was five years old, the future president began taking lessons from the tutor his father had hired to teach Thomas Randolph at Tuckahoe. It was the beginning of a fine education. He continued the lessons until 1752, when his parents decided to return to Shadwell with their growing family, including nine-year-old Thomas.

Upon their return, Peter Jefferson immediately began building. He built a much larger house for his family at Shadwell, as well as other structures to house slaves, cure tobacco, and protect the livestock. But young Thomas spent only his vacations and holidays at Shadwell. His father decided that his education came first, and to take it

Thomas Jefferson's schoolhouse

beyond the simple reading, writing, and arithmetic he had learned at Tuckahoe, Thomas was sent to Dover Church, about five miles away. At Dover, the Reverend William Douglas taught him Latin and some Greek and French. The young man also practiced the violin.

Thomas Jefferson continued his studies at Dover Church for five years. During that time, he made many visits to his home at Shadwell. There he was able to greet the many visitors who stopped on their journeys on Three Notch'd Road. Of all the guests, those he best remembered were the Cherokee Indians and their chief, Outassete.

Outassete, chief of the Cherokees

Outassete and the other Cherokees frequently made camp at Shadwell when they were traveling to or from Williamsburg, the capital of the Virginia Colony. Often, when the chief was visiting Peter Jefferson in the family's home, Thomas was a guest at the Indian camp. He particularly remembered a speech Outassete made when the warrior was planning to leave on a trip to England. "The moon was in full splendor," Thomas recalled years later, "and to her he seemed to address himself in his prayers for his own safety on the voyage, and that of his people during his absence." Thomas was mystified by Outassete's booming voice and graceful movements, as well as the silence of his followers gathered around the campfires. It made a great impression on him, even though, as he recalled more than half a century later, "I did not understand a word he uttered."

Jefferson continued his schooling at Dover Church and his frequent visits to Shadwell until he was a teenager. He grew tall and very thin, with broad shoulders and reddish hair. His friends began calling him "Long Tom." He learned the names of most of the trees and plants that grew in central Virginia. And he loved to read Homer and Virgil in Latin while canoeing lazily down the River Anna.

This carefree life came to an end on August 17, 1757, when Peter Jefferson died at the age of forty-nine. Thomas, only fourteen years old, suddenly became the oldest male in his family of six sisters and one baby brother. As he recalled later, the "whole care and direction of myself was thrown on myself entirely, without a relation or friend qualified to advise or guide me."

Despite the death of Peter Jefferson, the plantation system in Virginia allowed his family to continue growing and harvesting crops. Because slaves took care of the farming at Shadwell, Tom could continue his education at a church school in nearby Hanover. A few years later, he traveled by horseback 120 miles east to begin more schooling at William and Mary College in Williamsburg.

William and Mary College (above), founded in 1693, is the second oldest college in the country. William and Mary (below) were the rulers of Great Britain at the time the college was established.

Scenes along Duke of Gloucester Street in Williamsburg

When Thomas Jefferson entered college in March of 1760, the capital of Virginia Colony was a center of culture. Williamsburg did not yet have sidewalks or sewers, and grass grew on the town's half dozen roads. But along Duke of Gloucester Street, Williamsburg's main road, members of Virginia society met in homes, finer taverns, and the three or four buildings of William and Mary College.

As a student at William and Mary, Thomas was invited to many dinner parties, where he would often tell his favorite joke. The joke was about a person named Arthur Lee, who enjoyed arguing with people. According to Tom, Mr. Lee once heard a passerby say that it was a very cloudy day. "It is cloudy, sir," young Tom quoted Mr. Lee, "but not *very* cloudy." Tom thought this joke was quite funny, but whether others did is not known.

Life at college was not all parties, though. Few students at William and Mary studied harder than Thomas Jefferson. He quickly mastered difficult subjects such as Greek grammar, physics, and calculus. After little more than two years at the school, he had learned all that he could about the arts and sciences and moral philosophies. He left the college in April of 1762.

But even then, his studies were not complete. At the age of nineteen he began to study law in the Williamsburg law office of his friend George Wythe. Thomas, who had often made fun of the peculiar language of lawyers, now was forced to learn it.

Patrick Henry, a dramatic speaker, addresses the Virginia legislature.

While he was still a law student in the spring of 1764, he attended a meeting of the Virginia Colony legislature. While the delegates were arguing about a British law for taxing the colonies, an old friend named Patrick Henry rose to his feet. In an electrifying speech, Henry complained about the British government. Many of the other delegates shouted "Treason!" But young Tom Jefferson was impressed by Patrick Henry's words.

Three years later, in 1767, Tom completed his studies and became a lawyer. He didn't know it at the time, but it would soon become a dangerous job.

Jefferson's love for reading and writing is reflected in many of his inventions. Shown here are a comfortable chair with desktop attached (left) and an eight-sided, rotating table whose drawers are alphabetized files (below), both invented by Jefferson.

Chapter 3

More Than a Revolution

He had no love for the legal profession, but from the time he began practicing law in 1767, Thomas Jefferson was a very successful lawyer. His work grew from sixty-eight cases his first year to more than four hundred annually just a few years later. But he regarded a lawyer's work as part of the "dark side" of life. Reading and learning were far more important to him. Much of the money he earned as a lawyer he spent to buy books.

Most well-educated landholders in Virginia were expected to enter politics, and Jefferson did the same. He ran for the colonial Virginia legislature, called the House of Burgesses, and won easily in 1769. Every two years, he had to be reelected. To campaign, he just invited his neighbors to Shadwell, served them cake and rum punch, and waited for victory. It always came.

The main house at Monticello

The duties of a Virginia legislator under British rule were light. There was often time for other projects. Since his student days, Jefferson had dreamed of building a new home. It would be built on the highest point of his property, an 857-foot peak about a mile from Charlottesville. He called the hill *Monticello*, an Italian word meaning "little mountain." From the top, the view of the Piedmont Valley and the distant Blue Ridge Mountains was breathtaking.

Jefferson had just begun working on a little brick cottage at Monticello when a tragedy occurred. Early in 1770, Shadwell was destroyed by fire. Although his mother and sisters were not hurt, all of his books and papers were gone, as well as the building itself. Only his violin was saved by one of the servants. The family had no choice but to move to the unfinished little cottage at Monticello. In the meantime, Jefferson drew hundreds of detailed drawings of a great new mansion to be built on the "little mountain." He began spending even more of his income on books to replace those lost in the fire. Within a few years, he had put together a new library of more than a thousand volumes.

The same year that Shadwell burned to the ground, the twenty-seven-year-old lawyer met a beautiful young woman named Martha Wayles Skelton. Although only twenty-one years old, Martha was already a widow. Her first husband had died when she was only nineteen. When she returned to her wealthy family near Williamsburg, many of the young bachelors in Virginia called on her. Thomas Jefferson was one of them.

Thomas and Martha were married on New Year's Day, 1772. Despite a snowstorm that left up to three feet of snow on the ground, the newlyweds began the hundred-mile trip back to Monticello the same night. During the difficult journey, their carriage broke down and the pair finished the trip on horseback. When they finally reached Monticello, where the great new home was being built, it was night again. The bridegroom was careful not to awaken the sleeping servants as he led the horses to the stable.

Jefferson at Monticello with one of his slaves

Throughout his life, Thomas Jefferson dearly hoped for the chance to live a quiet family life at Monticello. He was an expert farmer, a fine architect and builder, well liked by his workers and even his slaves, and deeply in love with his new wife. But in the early 1770s, the fires of revolution were beginning to burn from Virginia to New England. For a young politician in colonial Virginia, quiet times at home were becoming difficult to find.

The Boston Massacre of 1770 infuriated the colonists.

As early as 1770, a large force of British soldiers had fired on angry protesters in Boston, killing five. The British charged a tax on tea that was hated throughout the colonies, because it was a symbol of British rule. All up and down the Atlantic seacoast, English officials were becoming more angry and violent.

In the fall of 1773, Jefferson helped to organize a group in the Virginia House of Burgesses. Called the Committee of Correspondence, it was set up to help the representatives of the thirteen colonies to communicate with one another and to unite against British rule.

The Boston Tea Party was meant to send a clear message of protest to the king of England.

The following spring, some residents of Boston, disguised as Indians, dumped a shipload of English tea into the ocean rather than pay a tax on it. Almost immediately, the British declared that Boston Harbor soon would be closed. To show their support for the people of Boston, the Virginia House of Burgesses voted in favor of a day of fasting and prayer.

The British governor of Virginia was so outraged that he dissolved the House of Burgesses the next day. However, Jefferson and the other leaders of the Virginia legislature continued to meet in Raleigh Tavern, just a few hundred feet from the Virginia capitol building in Williamsburg. There they called for the creation of a great

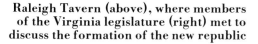
Raleigh Tavern (above), where members
of the Virginia legislature (right) met to
discuss the formation of the new republic

congress of all the colonies. Through the Committee of
Correspondence, they spread the word to the other colonies, stating "an attack on any one colony should be considered as an attack on the whole."

Each county in Virginia elected people who would
attend a meeting in Williamsburg to choose Virginia's
delegates to the new congress. Among the Virginians
elected were Jefferson, Patrick Henry, and George
Washington.

Before leaving home to attend the meeting, Jefferson
wrote a lengthy essay describing his feelings on the politics
of the day. Eventually published under the title "A Summary View of the Rights of British America," it was the
future president's first political masterpiece.

**King George III
of England**

In his essay, Jefferson asked why 160,000 voters in Great Britain "should give law to four millions in the States of America, every individual of whom is equal to every individual of them in virtue, in understanding, and in bodily strength." He continued with a long list of complaints about British rule in America. In reference to King George III of England, he suggested that kings "are the servants" of the people. Near the end of the essay, he wrote: "The God who gave us life, gave us liberty at the same time. . . ."

Because of an illness, Thomas Jefferson was not able to attend the Williamsburg meeting after all. But he sent one copy of his essay to Patrick Henry and another to Peyton Randolph, the chairman of the meeting. The copy sent to Patrick Henry was never seen again. Jefferson later wrote that Henry had either disliked it and thrown it away "or was too lazy to read it (for he was the laziest man in reading I ever knew). . . ." Fortunately, Peyton Randolph

The Old Ephrata Printing Press, on which the Declaration of Independence was printed

saved his copy and made it widely available. Some of the delegates were frightened by the language of Jefferson's document. They used more timid words to describe problems with the British. But the essay was printed and read by thousands of Americans. It was also read by the British government in England, where Jefferson was branded a criminal.

The first great meeting of all the colonies—called the First Continental Congress—met in Philadelphia in September 1774. Jefferson was still at Monticello then, getting over his illness. The Second Continental Congress began in May of the following year, right after the Battles of Lexington and Concord had started the revolutionary war. Many of the delegates were familiar with Jefferson's essay by now. His fine writing was one of the reasons he was selected to write the Declaration of Independence. So it was here that, on July 4, 1776—while Jefferson sat carefully recording the temperature—the great Declaration was signed.

Fac similes of the Signatures to the Declaration of Independence July 4 1776.

John Hancock and the signatures of the signers of the Declaration of Independence, including John Penn, Wm Floyd, John Hart, Wm Paca, Geo Read, Wm Hooper, Saml Adams, Geo Clymer, Step. Hopkins, Thos Nelson Jr., Charles Carroll of Carrollton, Wm Ellbridge Gerry, Thos M: Kean, Roger Sherman, Saml Huntington, Wm Whipple, Thomas Lynch Junr., Geo Taylor, Josiah Bartlett, Benj Franklin, Wm Williams, Richd Stockton, John Morton, Oliver Wolcott, Jno Witherspoon, Geo Ross, Thos Stone, Samuel Chase, Robt Treat Paine, George Wythe, Matthew Thornton, Frans Lewis, Th Jefferson, Benja Harrison, Lewis Morris, Abra Clark, Phil. Livingston, Casar Rodney, Arthur Middleton, Fras Hopkinson, Geo Walton, Carter Braxton, James Wilson, Richard Henry Lee, Thos Heyward Junr, Benjamin Rush, John Adams, Robt Morris, Lyman Hall, Joseph Hewes, Button Gwinnett, Francis Lightfoot Lee, William Ellery, Edward Rutledge, Jas Smith.

Department of State 19th April 1819. I Certify that this is a CORRECT Copy of the original Declaration of Independence deposited at this Department and that I have compared all the signatures with those of the original and have found them EXACT IMITATIONS. John Quincy Adams

**The signers of the Declaration of Independence (opposite page)
and their signatures (above)**

Jefferson left the Congress and returned to Virginia in September of 1776. He felt he had been away from home too long, for he had urgent business at the Virginia House of Delegates. This new group of legislators met in Williamsburg. As members of a revolutionary government, every delegate knew that he might well be put in prison if he were captured by British soldiers. But there was serious work to do.

Virginians were fighting to rid their land of the rule of the British king. Thomas Jefferson began a legal battle to turn Virginia into a true democracy. To do so, he needed the help of many of Virginia's political leaders. One of them, George Washington, had gone north to lead the American forces in battle against the British. Of the remaining leaders, the best known today is James Madison, a future president of the United States. Jefferson, Madison, and sometimes Patrick Henry and others worked to change Virginia laws. Little by little, the people of Virginia gained more equality and freedom.

The first great change Jefferson helped to make in Virginia law involved inheritance—what parents could leave to their children.

For centuries, English law said that the firstborn son in a family would inherit all the land owned by his father. This law, called "primogeniture," kept huge English estates from being broken up. But Jefferson regarded it as unfair, and helped write a law making it possible for families in Virginia to give land to more than one child. When this law was passed, it became possible for many more Virginians to become landowners.

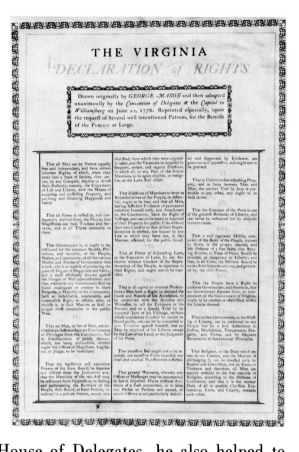

The Virginia Bill of Rights (1776). Virginia was the first state to incorporate a bill of rights into its constitution. Jefferson later urged the adoption of a bill of rights in the United States Constitution.

In the Virginia House of Delegates, he also helped to pass a law that made it possible for almost every freeman to get an education. But the law he was most proud of involved religious freedom. Jefferson felt that kings often used the church to make people obey them. "In every country and in every age," he wrote, "the priest has been hostile to liberty." Today these words may sound strange, and statements like that got Jefferson into some difficulties later in his life. But Virginia law, under Thomas Jefferson's constant prodding, became the first to be certain that government and religion were kept separate. Many of the ideas behind Virginia's new laws were used in the U.S. Constitution years later.

TO ALL BRAVE, HEALTHY, ABLE BODIED, AND WELL
DISPOSED YOUNG MEN,
IN THIS NEIGHBOURHOOD, WHO HAVE ANY INCLINATION TO JOIN THE TROOPS,
NOW RAISING UNDER
GENERAL WASHINGTON,
FOR THE DEFENCE OF THE
LIBERTIES AND INDEPENDENCE
OF THE UNITED STATES,
Against the hostile designs of foreign enemies,

TAKE NOTICE,

A public notice to enlist in Washington's revolutionary army

In 1779, Jefferson was elected governor of Virginia. Governor Jefferson was faced with terrible problems. The revolutionary war was raging throughout the northern colonies, and General George Washington desperately needed soldiers, supplies, and money to continue the battle. Jefferson gave almost all his horses and wagons to the American army. Many of his neighbors did the same.

In December of 1780, a huge fleet of British ships landed on the Virginia coast. British armies led by Benedict

46

Arnold, who had become the first American traitor, advanced deep into the interior and burned the capitol building in Richmond. After Jefferson had moved his family to a safer place, a British army captured Monticello. Surprisingly, they treated the home of the governor very well, damaging nothing before they left a few days later.

Because of the bravery of George Washington and the soldiers in the American army, and the considerable help of the French, the American Revolution was soon over. But there were Virginians who were frightened and angered by the British victories in Virginia. Although Jefferson had done what he could to protect his land, some thought that a dictator could better protect them in time of war. Many legislators wanted to appoint Patrick Henry or a general as Virginia's dictator. Because of the hard work of Jefferson and a few of his supporters, the move for a dictator was defeated "by a couple of votes."

Some people insisted on investigating Governor Jefferson for his conduct during the war. The investigation was ridiculous and was quickly dropped, but the future president was angered and saddened. He had done nothing to suggest that an investigation was needed. More importantly, he was shocked that Americans, fighting a bloody war to get rid of a king, were ready to appoint a dictator.

Jefferson would face the same battle again. Perhaps more than any other American, he helped to make the United States a democracy during its early years. He knew that the new nation needed more than a revolution. It needed a direction, a shining light that later generations could follow. At one point, he alone led the way.

Chapter 4

The Rough Road to Democracy

Thomas Jefferson retired as the governor of Virginia in the summer of 1781. In October, a huge army of British troops surrendered to General George Washington at Yorktown, Virginia. It was the last great battle of the American Revolution.

While America was winning its struggle for independence, Jefferson stayed at home in Monticello. At the request of the French government, he wrote a book called *Notes on the State of Virginia*. It is still read today by people interested in the early history of the United States and Virginia.

The summer of 1782 was the saddest time in Jefferson's life. His frail wife Martha, weakened after giving birth to her sixth child (three other children had died in infancy), was unable to recover her strength. When she finally died

A typical home interior in colonial Virginia

in September, her husband simply fell apart. During the final days of her life, Thomas promised never to marry again, and he never did. For six months after Martha's death, he stayed around Monticello, seeing no one but his children.

Toward the end of the year, members of the U.S. Congress asked Jefferson to travel to Europe to oversee a peace treaty with the British. Icy seas kept him from making the trip, but he at last seemed ready to work again. The Virginia legislature asked him to become a representative to the U.S. Congress, then meeting in Annapolis, Maryland, and he agreed. He attended Congress for half a year, sitting on most of the important committees.

Thomas Jefferson in 1786, at the age of forty-three

In May of 1784, Congress asked him to join John Adams and Benjamin Franklin as a minister to Europe. He accepted. The new job required him to develop trade agreements between the countries of Europe and the United States. With his oldest daughter, eleven-year-old Martha, he left for Europe in July.

"We had a lovely passage in a beautiful new ship," wrote Martha. "There were only six passengers, all of whom Papa knew, and a fine sunshine all the way, with a sea which was as calm as a river."

Thomas Jefferson and his daughter remained in Europe for five years. They visited many different countries. In England, he was treated rudely by the king and his officials. Many of them still regarded Jefferson as little more than a criminal.

The Constitutional Convention adopts the United States Constitution on September 17, 1787, in Philadelphia.

Always interested in science and agriculture, Jefferson found an extremely hardy kind of rice growing in Italy. When he tried to obtain some seeds so the new rice could be planted in America, he found that it was illegal to do so. Anyone caught taking rice out of the country, he was told, would be executed. Nevertheless, he filled his coat pockets with rice grains and hired someone to smuggle two sacks of it out of Italy.

The final two years of Jefferson's stay in Europe were historic times. Near the end of 1787, he received a copy of the new American Constitution. Although there were a number of things he liked about it, he was worried that it included no Bill of Rights. In a letter to James Madison, one of Virginia's delegates to the Constitutional Convention, Jefferson urged that a Bill of Rights be added. The first ten amendments to the Constitution (the Bill of Rights) were finally approved by Congress in 1791.

George Washington takes the oath of office as first president
of the United States at Federal Hall in New York City.

In 1789, the same year the American government was being formed according to the Constitution, the people of France revolted against the corrupt reign of their king, Louis XVI. A number of Frenchmen in the revolutionary government asked Thomas Jefferson to help them write a constitution for France. Although his French was excellent, Jefferson said that he could not do it. As a representative of the United States, he felt it would not be proper to help create the basic laws for a foreign nation.

America now had a Constitution of its own and, for the first time, a president. George Washington, like Jefferson, had been a delegate to the Continental Congress from Virginia. But while Jefferson had been writing the Declaration of Independence, Washington had gone north to lead the colonial forces against the British. Nevertheless, the two Virginians knew and respected each other.

George Washington and his cabinet. Left to right: Washington, Secretary of War Henry Knox, Secretary of the Treasury Alexander Hamilton, Secretary of State Thomas Jefferson, and Attorney General Edmund Randolph

Thomas Jefferson wrote to the new American president and asked for permission to return home. It was soon granted. Although Jefferson expected to return to his farming at Monticello, he immediately found that Washington had other plans. In November of 1789, Washington asked him to become secretary of state, an important office in the president's cabinet. Jefferson felt he could not refuse, but when he reached New York City, where the new government was meeting, he was shocked.

Alexander Hamilton's statue in front of the U.S. Treasury Building

Everywhere he met politicians who felt that the United States needed a king, not a democratically elected president. One of those politicians was Alexander Hamilton, Washington's secretary of the treasury. The common people were a "great beast," according to him. "Take mankind in general," Hamilton once said, "they are vicious." Even Vice-President John Adams felt that average Americans were unfit to participate in government. Of the important men in government, only Washington and Jefferson seemed to believe that all American freemen, including poor people, were capable of helping to govern themselves.

An anti-Jefferson cartoon showing him destroying the Federalist party with the aid of the devil

Throughout the time George Washington was president, politicians argued over what kind of government America should have. Some, especially Alexander Hamilton, believed government should be run by bankers, lawyers, and wealthy businessmen. Jefferson argued that as many different kinds of people as possible should take part in government. About the only thing the politicians could agree on was the establishment of a new American capital in Washington, D.C. For this to take place, a whole new city would have to be built on the Potomac River.

A cartoon that depicts Jefferson worshiping the mob rule of the French Revolution

For about a decade before Washington, D.C., was built, the government met in Philadelphia. There, the members of George Washington's cabinet continued their bitter arguments. Although Washington wanted to retire after his first term, the country was so divided politically that he was forced to run again. During Washington's second term, politicians argued even more bitterly.

Men like John Adams and Alexander Hamilton viewed the French Revolution with alarm. When the French king was killed, they thought it proved that common people did not deserve to be a part of a nation's government. Jefferson felt that the French government had been corrupt, and that the people of France had been kept extremely poor under the cruel king. Although France had been a great friend to America during the American Revolution, many people, including Adams and Hamilton, hated the new French government.

John Adams, second president of the United States. Enemies during much of their political careers, he and Jefferson became friends in later years, after the death of Jefferson's daughter Mary.

By the end of his second term, George Washington was tired of all the arguments in his cabinet. He refused to run for a third term. Vice-President John Adams, who in some respects thought a president should be like a king, decided to run for president. Almost as an afterthought, friends of Jefferson urged him to run against Adams.

Jefferson was reluctant to run, but finally agreed. Probably because Jefferson did little campaigning, John Adams won in a close election. According to the rules of the time, Jefferson, who had received the second most electoral votes for the presidency, became America's new vice-president.

On March 4, 1797, fifty-three-year-old Thomas Jefferson was sworn in as the vice-president of the United States. President Adams and Vice-President Jefferson were extremely different personalities. Adams, a member of the Federalist party, believed that the nation's business was best taken care of by people in the upper class. Jefferson, a member of the Republican party (which later became today's Democratic party) believed that common people were capable of governing themselves.

In 1798, Federalists in Congress passed laws called the Alien and Sedition Acts. Even as the president of the Senate, Jefferson could do little to stop the passage of laws he was sure went against the First Amendment of the U.S. Constitution. The Sedition Act made it possible to put people in jail for criticizing the U.S. government. The Alien Act allowed the president to exile anyone he judged to be dangerous to the United States.

The First Amendment to the Constitution says that Congress shall pass no law limiting the American people's freedom of speech. Jefferson knew that the Alien and Sedition Acts were clearly against the Constitution. These laws soon allowed what he called a "Federalist reign of terror." The first person put in jail under the law was a U.S. congressman from Vermont named Matthew Lyon. Lyon was arrested and sentenced to four months in prison for saying, among other things, that President Adams seemed to live like a king.

Many other people were soon put in jail under the harsh terms of the Sedition Act. Thomas Jefferson was angered by the cruel law. As the eighteenth century drew to a close, he began inspiring others to work against the unconstitutional acts. He also began the campaign that would make him the third president of the United States.

Thomas Jefferson's face peers from many articles of currency issued by the United States over the years. Above: Not a postage stamp, but a bill of fractional currency, or postal currency, issued in 1861. Stamps were once used as money but were often too sticky to be practical. Bills that look like stamps were issued to replace them.

Right: The Jefferson nickel, designed by Felix Schlag of Chicago, replaced the buffalo nickel in 1938. Opposite page, top to bottom: (1) This Series 1976 $2 bill shows the signing of the Declaration of Independence on one side and Jefferson's portrait on the other. (2) A Series 1880 $2 bill (3) A $2 bill issued by the Federal Reserve Bank of Chicago in 1914, when certain banks were allowed to issue their own currency

Washington, D.C., as it looked in 1800

Chapter 5

The Third President

In the year 1800, Thomas Jefferson began his campaign for the presidency at the age of fifty-seven. He felt forced to do so.

At the start of the nineteenth century, America was badly divided. Most of the wealthy landowners and businessmen in the country were Federalists. The Sedition Act made it extremely dangerous to criticize Federalist policies. Republicans, often poor or middle-class people with little property, believed that Thomas Jefferson was the most influential man in America who spoke for their interests.

Although Jefferson believed in the rights and abilities of the common people, he seldom made speeches to them. He began his campaign by writing letters to local politicians and newspapers all across the nation. He urged people to organize a Republican campaign at the local level.

In the spring of 1800, Republican congressmen nominated Thomas Jefferson for president. For his running mate, a former senator from New York named Aaron Burr was selected. The event marked the start of one of the dirtiest presidential campaigns in the history of the United States.

Religious leaders in New England and even Virginia were quick to criticize the Republican candidate for wanting to keep religion and politics separate. If America elected Thomas Jefferson, said the Reverend John M. Mason, it would show a "disregard of the religion of Jesus Christ." The *New England Palladium* newspaper reported that if Jefferson were elected, "the seal of death is that moment set on our holy religion." Many preachers in New England called him the "Antichrist," or the enemy of Jesus. For three decades, the Philadelphia Public Library refused to keep any books based on the writings or life of Thomas Jefferson.

As Jefferson himself had warned earlier, religious leaders seemed more than willing to help the cause of politicians in power.

To his credit, President John Adams, the Federalist candidate, refused to criticize Jefferson's stand on religion. He insisted instead that the Republican candidate was "a good patriot citizen and father." Jefferson himself refused to discuss his religious views publicly. But some Federalist politicians were more than willing to criticize him in public. They called him a drunkard, a coward, a slave driver, a mad scientist, the devil, and a worshiper of the uneducated masses.

Aaron Burr,
Jefferson's
vice-president,
caused him no
end of problems.

In the end, it was the masses who elected Jefferson over Adams. As Abraham Lincoln noted half a century later, "God must love the common people because He made so many of them." There simply were not enough wealthy Federalists to win the election for John Adams. But there was a peculiar twist to the contest. Although all Republicans had assumed that Jefferson was running for president and Aaron Burr for vice-president, the number of electoral votes for each was the same.

Suddenly, it was possible for Aaron Burr, whom many distrusted, including Jefferson, to become president! According to the Constitution, the question had to be settled in the House of Representatives.

Highly Important and Interesting.

PENNSYLVANIA.   PHILAD. FEB. 14.
BY EXPRESS.
WASHINGTON, Feb. 11, half past 3, afternoon.

"ACCORDING to the rule of proceedings established by the House, they proceeded to the Senate Chamber, where (by Mr. *Nicholas* and Mr. *Rutledge*, the tellers on the part of the House, and Mr. *Wells* on the part of the Senate) the votes were counted and the result declared by the Vice-President, as follow :—

For THOMAS JEFFERSON,	73
AARON BURR,	73
JOHN ADAMS,	65
C. C. PINCKNEY,	64
JOHN JAY,	1

The tellers declared there was some informality in the votes of *Georgia*, but believing them to be the true votes, reported them as such.

The Vice-President then, in pursuance of the duty enjoined upon him, declared, that *Thomas Jefferson* and *Aaron Burr* being equal in the number of Votes, it remained for the House of Representatives to determine the choice.

The two Houses then separated, and the House of Representatives returned to their chamber, where seats had been previously prepared for the members of the Senate. A call of the members of the House, arranged according to States, was then made; upon which it appeared, that every member was present except Gen. *Sumpter*, who is unwell, and unable to attend. Mr. *Nicholson* of *Maryland*, was also unwell but attended and had a bed prepared for him in one of the committee rooms, to which place the ballot box was carried to him, by the tellers appointed on the part of the State.

The mode of balloting was this—each State had a ballot box in which the members belonging to it, having previously appointed a teller, put the votes of the State; the teller on the part of the United States, having then counted the votes, duplicates of the result were put by him into two general ballot boxes—Tellers being nominated by each State for the purpose of examining the general ballot boxes, they were divided into two parts, of whom one examined one of the general ballot boxes, and the other examining the other.—Upon comparing the result and finding them to agree, the votes were stated to the Speaker who declared them to the House.

The first ballot was 8 States for JEFFERSON, 6 for BURR, and 2 divided.

Which result continues to be the same, although they have already balloted seven times. A motion was made about half an hour since, to repeat the ballot in one hour, and was agreed to. The balloting is to recommence at the expiration of that time. Some of the members have gone to their lodgings to dine, and others are taking refreshments in the Committee Rooms.

As there will be no possibility of ascertaining what will be the event of the choice to be made by the House for some time to come, it is not improbable that the balloting will continue for some days. *Yours, &c.*

"3 o'clock A. M. Two ballots have been taken since :—The same result.—Ballot to be repeated again at 4 o'clock."   [*Thus far our Correspondent.*]

At the request of the Speaker the mail was detained until 4, on Thursday morning, that the members might have an opportunity of communicating these proceedings.

The ballot which was to take place at 4, made the TWENTY-FIRST essay of the House to come to a decision.

An announcement of the tie between presidential candidates Thomas Jefferson and Aaron Burr

Angry that their candidate had lost, many Federalist congressmen decided to vote for Aaron Burr instead of Jefferson. Fortunately, Alexander Hamilton, a Federalist and no friend of Jefferson, saved the day by throwing his support toward the Virginian. After a week of tied votes, Jefferson was finally elected president by the House of Representatives on February 17, 1801. Aaron Burr became vice-president.

Jefferson arrives in the new capital of Washington, D.C., for his inauguration.

On March 5, 1801, the day he was sworn into office, the new president began to heal the wounds of a divided nation. "We are all Republicans—we are all Federalists," he said in his quiet speech. "Sometimes it is said that man cannot be trusted with the government of himself. Can he then be trusted with the government of others? Or have we found angels in the forms of kings to govern him? Let history answer this question."

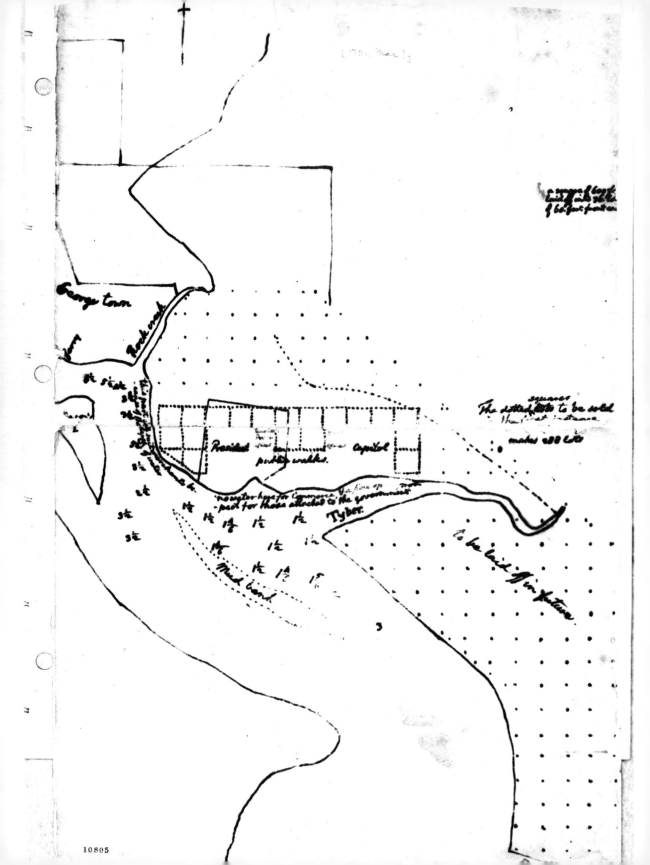

George town

Rock creek

President

public walks.

Capitol

Tyber

Mud bank

The dotted squares to be sold the first instance

makes 288 lots

To be laid off in future

10805

Opposite page: Jefferson's sketched map of Washington, D.C.
Above: The White House in 1807

In the summer of 1800, Washington, D.C., had become the new capital of the United States. Although the President's House (forerunner of the White House) and the Capitol Building had been completed in 1800, Jefferson began his presidency in a swampy new town with no real streets or sidewalks. There was just a scattering of small houses for members of the U.S. government to live in. Jefferson became the first U.S. president to begin his term in the building known as the White House.

The new president quickly demonstrated that he regarded all people as equals. When former President John Adams had invited people to dinner, he had sat at the head of a table and had carefully seated all the other guests. Those he considered most important and most powerful were seated first, usually closest to the president. Others were seated in the order of their supposed importance.

Jefferson held his dinners at a round table, so no one could sit at the head. Instead of seating people in a careful order, he encouraged the women to scramble for their seats first, followed by the men. Some of his guests, used to different arrangements, were outraged. "Nobody shall be above you, nor you above anybody," he told them.

When he was working on his first speech to Congress, Jefferson wrote that the Sedition Act was unconstitutional. When he gave the speech, however, he struck out the passage. Although he hated the law, he was anxious not to anger Federalist politicians. He wanted a united America. But he worked to end the law in other ways. He tried to impeach—or throw out of office—a Federalist judge who was in favor of the Sedition Act. Although the effort failed, many judges began to realize that the mood of the nation had shifted against the Sedition Act. Most grew wary of enforcing it.

More than in any other way, Jefferson showed his lack of support for the law by personal example. There were many newspapers in the U.S. that favored the Federalist point of view. Some of them printed vicious criticisms of the Republican president. But even when the stories were lies, Jefferson took no action against the newspapers. He regarded freedom of the press as more important than his personal feelings. Many historians see Jefferson's support of a free press as one of his most lasting contributions.

His other great contribution occurred in 1803. Throughout his administration, Jefferson tried hard to avoid political problems with Europeans. But in 1803, two of the most powerful nations in Europe, England and France, began an all-out war. Under Emperor Napoleon Bonaparte, France was trying to conquer much of Europe. It had also acquired a vast amount of territory in the New World. In 1800, France had secretly obtained the land called Louisiana from Spain. Today, Louisiana is just one state. But in the early 1800s, the territory called Louisiana included most of the land between the Mississippi River and the Rocky Mountains—a vast amount of land.

Jefferson learned about the secret deal in 1801. He was greatly alarmed. Spain, the old owner of Louisiana, was no longer a great military power. But under Napoleon, France was a warlike nation. With a great fleet of ships under his command, Napoleon could easily send a large army to New Orleans, at the mouth of the Mississippi River, to take charge of Louisiana. The troops might endanger river traffic on the Mississippi, America's western highway.

By 1803, Jefferson was facing a terrible decision. He knew that the American army was no match for Napoleon's. If French troops landed in Louisiana, the only way to fight them would be to make an alliance with Great Britain, a nation he did not trust. The day French soldiers arrived in New Orleans, he told his advisers, "we must marry ourselves to the British fleet and nation."

Jefferson signing the Louisiana Purchase papers

The president began to act on a secret plan. He decided to try to buy the vast territory called Louisiana from the French. Secretly, he asked Congress to approve a $2 million fund for business matters with "foreign nations" that were not specified. In March of 1803 he sent James Monroe to France to try to buy Louisiana from Napoleon. The emperor, in need of money to finance his wars, was more than ready to make a deal. On May 2, he sold the entire Louisiana Territory to the United States for sixty million francs, about $15 million.

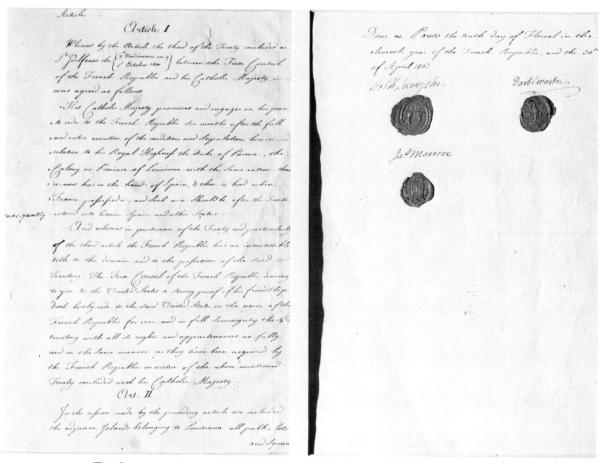

The Louisiana Purchase document

The Louisiana Purchase was the largest real estate deal in history. On May 2, 1803, the size of the United States was doubled! Today, the land that Thomas Jefferson so wisely purchased includes the states of Arkansas, Iowa, Kansas, Louisiana, Minnesota, Missouri, Montana, Nebraska, North Dakota, Oklahoma, South Dakota, and Wyoming. Overnight, the United States became one of the largest countries in the world, larger than all the nations of western Europe combined.

Army officers Meriwether Lewis (left) and William Clark (right) met with Indians (above) as they made their way through the Northwest territory in search of a passage to the Pacific Ocean.

Ever since he became president, Jefferson had wanted to have America's Northwest territory explored. He believed a route could be found across North America to the Pacific Ocean. He also wanted information on the plants, animals, and Indians of the region. Now, with the lands of the Louisiana Purchase under American control, he could carry out his plans. Jefferson chose two army officers, Meriwether Lewis and William Clark, to lead an expedition.

The Shoshoni Indian Sacajawea (meaning "Bird Woman") guiding Lewis and Clark through the Rocky Mountains

Lewis and Clark set off on their journey in May 1804. They were soon joined by a trader, Toussaint Charbonneau, and his Shoshoni Indian wife, Sacajawea, who helped them find their way through the wilderness and deal with Indians along the way. The notebooks and drawings Lewis and Clark made tell of many adventures and discoveries: fierce grizzly bears, the majestic Rocky Mountains, vast prairies and forests, and new Indian tribes. Although their route to the Pacific proved too rough to be practical for trade, the expedition helped open up the Northwest to settlers and gain the Oregon territory for the United States.

Above: Part of the letter Lewis wrote to Clark inviting him to join the Northwest expedition. Lewis tells Clark that "there is no man on earth" he would rather have join him on the expedition than Clark.

Left: A page from one of Clark's notebooks, describing a trout. He says the fish is "superior to any fish I ever tasted" and is "best when cooked in Indian style," on a wooden spit.

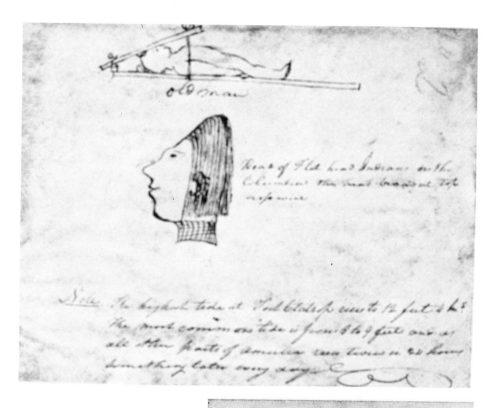

Above: Clark's notebook entry on the Flathead Indians he encountered near the Columbia River. The top drawing shows how an infant's head was flattened using boards.
Right: Clark's drawing of a bird he called the "cock of the plains," observed in the region of the Rocky Mountains

Aaron Burr killed Alexander Hamilton in a duel at Weehawkin, New Jersey, on July 11, 1804. A fugitive from justice in both New York and New Jersey, Burr then headed to the South and the West and schemed to set up an empire there. He was tried for treason in 1807, but was acquitted.

By the time the next presidential election came in 1804, Jefferson was extraordinarily popular. Although a few Federalist politicians and newspapers still howled against him, most Americans were solidly behind the president and his policies. The same could not be said for Vice-President Aaron Burr.

For years, Burr and Alexander Hamilton had been feuding. Hamilton often publicly insulted the vice-president. Finally, Burr challenged Hamilton to a duel and killed him on July 11, 1804, in New Jersey. Soon, authorities in both New York and New Jersey were preparing to arrest the vice-president of the United States for murder!

Not surprisingly, Jefferson no longer wanted Burr as his vice-president. Instead, the nomination went to George Clinton, the governor of New York State. Jefferson and Clinton easily won. Of the seventeen states then part of the U.S., fifteen went to Jefferson. The Federalists were all but destroyed. Even former President John Adams, no friend of the Republicans, voted for Jefferson.

Martha Jefferson Randolph, Thomas's oldest child, was the only one of his six children who lived a long life.

It was a smashing victory, but not one that the sixty-one-year-old president could enjoy for long. In the spring, his twenty-six-year-old daughter Mary fell seriously ill. The president rushed to Monticello just in time to be at her side when she died. Of the six children born to Thomas and Martha Jefferson, only one daughter, Martha, remained alive. The president completed his second term under a cloud of sorrow.

Throughout that second term, much of Jefferson's energies were taken up trying to keep America out of the war raging between England and France. He succeeded by fighting an economic war, refusing to trade with a number of European nations, especially Great Britain. His policies cost shippers and businessmen millions of dollars and were very controversial.

By the end of 1807, he announced that he would follow the example of George Washington and not seek a third term. The administration of one of America's greatest presidents had come to an end.

Chapter 6

The Sage of Monticello

On March 4, 1809, James Madison was sworn in as the fourth president of the United States. It was exactly as Jefferson had wished. He had worked hard to help Madison become the new president.

Just before the inauguration ceremony, Madison asked him to ride to the Capitol in the new president's coach. Jefferson thanked him but declined. "I wished," he said, "not to divide with him the honors of the day." Instead, he rode a horse alone to the Capitol, hitched it to a post, and walked up the long steps. One week later, he rode in a coach piled high with luggage toward Monticello. He would never return to Washington.

Along much of the journey, people greeted him kindly. When he finally arrived at his hilltop home, he was greeted by many of his neighbors.

Although he was now sixty-six years old, the ex-president began a new life at Monticello, filled with energy. He rose every morning at dawn and built a fire. Then he would read and write until breakfast, after which he would ride miles on horseback looking after the many interests at Monticello. After dinner, he spent the remainder of the day reading and answering letters.

In his retirement, Thomas Jefferson was the most famous living American. In an average year he received more than a thousand letters, most of which he tried to answer. Every year, thousands of visitors flocked to Monticello to meet with the ex-president. He maintained beds for fifty overnight guests, but on many occasions they were not enough for the crowds who came to see him. Feeding the visitors was often extremely expensive, but he took care to do so, nevertheless.

Right: The dumbwaiter that Jefferson built to carry bottles of wine up to his dining room from his wine cellar in the basement Opposite page: Jefferson's polygraph, a device for writing two copies of a letter at the same time

His many interests and talents were put to good use at Monticello. He invented an ingenious device that opened both double doors to his parlor when just one of them was pushed. The chain and iron wheels that performed the movement still work perfectly today. He built the first dumbwaiter in America—a kind of tiny, hand-operated elevator that brought up bottles of wine from his cellar. He invented dozens of other devices, including an improved plow and a device that allowed him to write two identical letters at the same time.

The rotunda of the University of Virginia in Charlottesville,
designed by Jefferson

In 1812, he received a letter from ex-President John
Adams, who was retired in Massachusetts. The two men
had once been friends, but had not talked to each other
since the Federalist-Republican squabbles around the turn
of the century. Beginning in 1812, the two ex-presidents
wrote lengthy letters to one another. Historians still study
these letters today.

In 1817, when he was seventy-four years old, Jefferson
began working on one of his greatest achievements. For
years, he had been planning a system of education for
Virginians. It included free elementary schools, high
schools, and a great new university. By the following year,

A life mask of Jefferson, made in 1825, one year before his death

he had convinced the Virginia legislature to provide $45,000 to help educate poor elementary students, and $15,000 to begin building the University of Virginia. He insisted that the university be built in Charlottesville, not far from Monticello.

The Virginia state legislators didn't want to give much money to the new university. But year after year, Jefferson rode to the state capital and asked for more money for the great project. When he was not raising funds, he designed the red brick buildings and helped to build them. When he could not find skilled builders, he taught laborers how to lay bricks and do carpentry work. By the time the main buildings of the new University of Virginia were finished in 1825, he had collected, and spent, about $300,000.

Knowing that a great university required great teachers, he sent assistants around Europe in search of scholars willing to travel to America and teach at the University of Virginia. When it opened in 1825, Jefferson concluded that it was one of the great achievements of his life.

Jefferson's bedroom, in which he died

The following year was his last. At the age of eighty-three his vast energies were finally beginning to fail. Although he had only one living daughter, he was surrounded by family in his final days. His daughter, Martha, had eleven children. Many of these children also had children, so the old president had many great-grandchildren. On July 3, 1826, he lay dying in bed. He desperately wanted to live just one more day. Somehow, he made it through the night.

On the next day Jefferson's old friend John Adams, the second president of the United States, died in Massachusetts. Early that afternoon of July 4, 1826, Thomas Jefferson, the third president of the United States, also died. To the very day, the nation his hand had declared independent was half a century old.

LETTER from THOMAS JEFFERSON,

To Mr. WEIGHTMAN, late Mayor of Washington.

Monticello, June 24th, 1826.

RESPECTED SIR:

The kind invitation I receive from you, on the part of the citizens of the city of Washington, to be present with them at their celebration on the fiftieth anniversary of American Independence, as one of the surviving signers of an instrument pregnant with our own, and the fate of the world, is most flattering to myself, and heightened by the honorable accompaniment proposed for the comfort of such a journey. It adds sensibly to the sufferings of sickness, to be deprived by it of a personal participation in the rejoicings of that day. But acquiescence is a duty, under circumstances not placed among those we are permitted to control. I should indeed, with peculiar delight, have met and exchanged there congratulations personally with the small band, the remnant of that host of worthies, who joined with us on that day, in the bold and doubtful election we were to make for our country, between submission or the sword; and to have enjoyed with them the consolatory fact, that our fellow citizens, after half a century of experience and prosperity, continue to approve the choice we made. May it be to the world, what I believe it will be, (to some parts sooner, to others later, but finally to all,) the signal of arousing men to burst the chains under which monkish ignorance and superstition had pursuaded them to bind themselves, and to assume the blessings and security of self-government. That form which we have substituted, restores the free right to the unbounded exercise of reason and freedom of opinion. All eyes are opened, or opening to the rights of man.— The general spread of the light of science has already laid open to every view the palpable truth, that the mass of mankind has not been born with saddles on their backs, nor a favored few, booted and spurred, ready to ride them legitimately, by the grace of God. These are grounds of hope for others. For ourselves, let the annual return of this day, forever refresh our recollections of these rights, and an undiminished devotion to them.

I will ask permission here to express the pleasure with which I should have met my antient neighbours of the city of Washington and its vicinities, with whom I passed so many years of a pleasing social intercourse; an intercourse which so much relieved the anxieties of the public cares, and left impressions so deeply engraved in my affections, as never to be forgotten. With my regret that ill health forbids me the gratification of an acceptance, be pleased to receive for yourself, and those for whom you write, the assurance of my highest respect and friendly attachments.

TH: JEFFERSON.

Jefferson turned down an invitation for a celebration
that would take place on the day of his death.

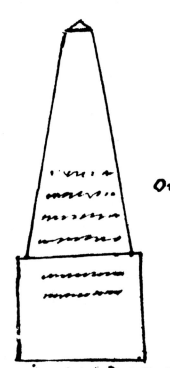

could the dead feel any interest in Monu
-ments or other remembrances of them, when, as
Anacreon says. Ολιγη δε κεισομεσθα
                  Κονις, οσεων λυθεντων
the following would be to my Manes the most
gratifying.
On the grave
        a plain die or cube of 3.f without any
mouldings, surmounted by an Obelisk
of 6.f. height, each of a single stone:
on the faces of the Obelisk the following
inscription, & not a word more.
        Here was buried
        Thomas Jefferson
Author of the Declaration of American Independance
        of the Statute of Virginia for religious freedom
& Father of the University of Virginia.

because by these, as testimonials that I have lived, I wish most to
be remembered. to be of the coarse stone of which
my columns are made, that no one might be tempted
hereafter to destroy it for the value of the materials.
my bust by Ciracchi, with the pedestal and truncated
column on which it stands, might be given to the University
if they would place it in the Dome room of the Rotunda.
on the Die of the Obelisk might be engraved
        Born apr. 2. 1743. O.S.
        Died ——   ,

Above: The instructions Jefferson wrote regarding his tombstone
Opposite page: Jefferson's tombstone at Monticello

Chronology of American History

(Shaded area covers events in Thomas Jefferson's lifetime.)

About A.D. 982 — Eric the Red, born in Norway, reaches Greenland in one of the first European voyages to North America.

About 985 — Eric the Red brings settlers from Iceland to Greenland.

About 1000 — Leif Ericson (Eric the Red's son) leads what is thought to be the first European expedition to mainland North America; Leif probably lands in Canada.

1492 — Christopher Columbus, hoping to find a sea route from Spain to the Far East, discovers the New World.

1497 — John Cabot reaches Canada in the first English voyage to North America.

1513 — Ponce de Léon explores Florida in search of the fabled Fountain of Youth.

1519-1521 — Hernando Cortés of Spain conquers Mexico.

1534 — French explorers led by Jacques Cartier enter the Gulf of St. Lawrence in Canada.

1540 — Spanish explorer Francisco Coronado begins exploring the American Southwest, seeking the riches of the mythical Seven Cities of Cibola.

1565 — St. Augustine, Florida, the first permanent European town in what is now the United States, is founded by the Spanish.

1607 — Jamestown, Virginia, is founded, the first permanent English town in the present-day U.S.

1608 — Frenchman Samuel de Champlain founds the village of Quebec, Canada.

1609 — Henry Hudson explores the eastern coast of present-day U.S. for the Netherlands; the Dutch then claim parts of New York, New Jersey, Delaware, and Connecticut and name the area New Netherland.

1619 — The English colonies' first shipment of black slaves arrives in Jamestown.

1620 — English Pilgrims found Massachusetts' first permanent town at Plymouth.

1621 — Massachusetts Pilgrims and Indians hold the famous first Thanksgiving feast in colonial America.

1623 — Colonization of New Hampshire is begun by the English.

1624 — Colonization of present-day New York State is begun by the Dutch at Fort Orange (Albany).

1625 — The Dutch start building New Amsterdam (now New York City).

1630 — The town of Boston, Massachusetts, is founded by the English Puritans.

1633 — Colonization of Connecticut is begun by the English.

1634 — Colonization of Maryland is begun by the English.

1636 — Harvard, the colonies' first college, is founded in Massachusetts.

1636 — Rhode Island colonization begins when Englishman Roger Williams founds Providence.

1638 — Delaware colonization begins when Swedish people build Fort Christina at present-day Wilmington.

1640 — Stephen Daye of Cambridge, Massachusetts prints *The Bay Psalm Book*, the first English-language book published in what is now the U.S.

1643 — Swedish settlers begin colonizing Pennsylvania.

About 1650 — North Carolina is colonized by Virginia settlers.

1660 — New Jersey colonization is begun by the Dutch at present-day Jersey City.

1670 — South Carolina colonization is begun by the English near Charleston.

1673 — Jacques Marquette and Louis Jolliet explore the upper Mississippi River for France.

1682—Philadelphia, Pennsylvania, is settled.

1682—La Salle explores Mississippi River all the way to its mouth in Louisiana and claims the whole Mississippi Valley for France.

1693—College of William and Mary is founded in Williamsburg, Virginia.

1700—Colonial population is about 250,000.

1703—Benjamin Franklin is born in Boston.

1732—George Washington, first president of the U.S., is born in Westmoreland County, Virginia.

1733—James Oglethorpe founds Savannah, Georgia; Georgia is established as the thirteenth colony.

1735—John Adams, second president of the U.S., is born in Braintree, Massachusetts.

1737—William Byrd founds Richmond, Virginia.

1738—British troops are sent to Georgia over border dispute with Spain.

1739—Black insurrection takes place in South Carolina.

1740—English Parliament passes act allowing naturalization of immigrants to American colonies after seven-year residence.

1743—Thomas Jefferson, third president of the U.S., is born in Albemarle County, Virginia. Benjamin Franklin retires at age thirty-seven to devote himself to scientific inquiries and public service.

1744—King George's War begins; France joins war effort against England.

1745—During King George's War, France raids settlements in Maine and New York.

1747—Classes begin at Princeton College in New Jersey.

1748—The Treaty of Aix-la-Chapelle concludes King George's War.

1749—Parliament legally recognizes slavery in colonies and the inauguration of the plantation system in the south. George Washington becomes the surveyor for Culpepper County in Virginia.

1750—Thomas Walker passes through and names Cumberland Gap on his way toward Kentucky region. Colonial population is about 1,200,000.

1751—James Madison, fourth president of the U.S., is born in Port Conway, Virginia. English Parliament passes Currency Act, banning New England colonies from issuing paper money. George Washington travels to Barbados.

1752—Pennsylvania Hospital, the first general hospital in the colonies, is founded in Philadelphia. Benjamin Franklin uses a kite in a thunderstorm to demonstrate that lightning is a form of electricity.

1753—George Washington delivers command from Virginia Lieutenant Governor Dinwiddie that the French withdraw from the Ohio River Valley; French disregard the demand. Colonial population is about 1,328,000.

1754—French and Indian War begins (extends to Europe as the Seven Years' War). Washington surrenders at Fort Necessity.

1755—French and Indians ambush General Braddock. Washington becomes commander of Virginia troops.

1756—England declares war on France.

1758—James Monroe, fifth president of the U.S., is born in Westmoreland County, Virginia.

1759—Cherokee Indian war begins in southern colonies; hostilities extend to 1761. George Washington marries Martha Dandridge Custis.

1760—George III becomes king of England. Colonial population is about 1,600,000.

1762—England declares war on Spain.

1763—Treaty of Paris concludes the French and Indian War and the Seven Years' War. England gains Canada and most other French lands east of the Mississippi River.

1764—British pass the Sugar Act to gain tax money from the colonists. The issue of taxation without representation is first introduced in Boston. John Adams marries Abigail Smith.

1765—Stamp Act goes into effect in the colonies. Business virtually stops as almost all colonists refuse to use the stamps.

1766—British repeal the Stamp Act.

1767—John Quincy Adams, sixth president of the U.S. and son of second president John Adams, is born in Braintree, Massachusetts.

1769—Daniel Boone sights the Kentucky territory.

1770—In the Boston Massacre, British soldiers kill five colonists and injure six. Townshend Acts are repealed, thus eliminating all duties on imports to the colonies except tea.

1771—Benjamin Franklin begins his autobiography, a work that he will never complete. The North Carolina assembly passes the "Bloody Act," which makes rioters guilty of treason.

1772—Samuel Adams rouses colonists to consider British threats to self-government. Thomas Jefferson marries Martha Wayles Skelton.

1773—English Parliament passes the Tea Act. Colonists dressed as Mohawk Indians board British tea ships and toss 342 casks of tea into the water in what becomes known as the Boston Tea Party.

1774—British close the port of Boston to punish the city for the Boston Tea Party. First Continental Congress convenes in Philadelphia.

1775—American Revolution begins with battles of Lexington and Concord, Massachusetts. Second Continental Congress opens in Philadelphia. George Washington becomes commander-in-chief of the Continental army.

1776—Declaration of Independence is adopted on July 4.

1777—Congress adopts the American flag with thirteen stars and thirteen stripes. John Adams is sent to France to negotiate peace treaty.

1778—France declares war against Great Britain and becomes U.S. ally.

1779—British surrender to Americans at Vincennes. Thomas Jefferson is elected governor of Virginia. James Madison is elected to the Continental Congress.

1780—Benedict Arnold, first American traitor, defects to the British.

1781—Articles of Confederation go into effect. Cornwallis surrenders to George Washington at Yorktown, ending the American Revolution.

1782—American commissioners, including John Adams, sign peace treaty with British in Paris. Thomas Jefferson's wife, Martha, dies.

1785—Congress adopts the dollar as the unit of currency. John Adams is made minister to Great Britain. Thomas Jefferson is appointed minister to France.

1786—Shays' Rebellion begins in Massachusetts.

1787—Constitutional Convention assembles in Philadelphia to revise Articles of Confederation; U.S. Constitution is adopted. Delaware, New Jersey, and Pennsylvania become states.

1788—Virginia, South Carolina, New York, Connecticut, New Hampshire, Maryland, and Massachusetts become states. U.S. Constitution is ratified. New York City is declared temporary U.S. capital.

1789—Presidential electors elect George Washington and John Adams as first president and vice-president. Thomas Jefferson is appointed secretary of state. North Carolina becomes a state. French Revolution begins.

1790—Supreme Court meets for the first time. Rhode Island becomes a state. First national census in the U.S. counts 3,929,214 persons.

1791—Vermont enters the Union. U.S. Bill of Rights, the first ten amendments to the Constitution, goes into effect. District of Columbia is established.

1792—Thomas Paine publishes *The Rights of Man*. Kentucky becomes a state. Two political parties are formed in the U.S., Federalist and Republican. Washington is elected to a second term, with Adams as vice-president.

1793—War between France and Britain begins; U.S. declares neutrality. Eli Whitney invents the cotton gin; cotton production and slave labor increase in the South.

1794—Eleventh Amendment to the Constitution is passed, limiting federal courts' power. "Whiskey Rebellion" in Pennsylvania protests federal whiskey tax. James Madison marries Dolley Payne Todd.

1795—George Washington signs the Jay Treaty with Great Britain. Treaty of San Lorenzo, between U.S. and Spain, settles Florida boundary and gives U.S. right to navigate the Mississippi.

1796—Tennessee enters the Union. Washington gives his Farewell Address, refusing a third presidential term. John Adams is elected president and Thomas Jefferson vice-president.

1797—Adams recommends defense measures against possible war with France. Napoleon Bonaparte and his army march against Austrians in Italy. U.S. population is about 4,900,000.

1798—Washington is named commander-in-chief of the U.S. army. Department of the Navy is created. Alien and Sedition Acts are passed. Napoleon's troops invade Egypt and Switzerland.

1799—George Washington dies at Mount Vernon. James Monroe is elected governor of Virginia. French Revolution ends. Napoleon becomes ruler of France.

1800—Thomas Jefferson and Aaron Burr tie for president. U.S. capital is moved from Philadelphia to Washington, D.C. The White House is built as presidents' home. Spain returns Louisiana to France.

1801—After thirty-six ballots, House of Representatives elects Thomas Jefferson president, making Burr vice-president. James Madison is named secretary of state.

1802—Congress abolishes excise taxes. U.S. Military Academy is founded at West Point, New York.

1803—Ohio enters the Union. Louisiana Purchase treaty is signed with France, greatly expanding U.S. territory.

1804—Twelfth Amendment to the Constitution rules that president and vice-president be elected separately. Alexander Hamilton is killed by Vice-President Aaron Burr in a duel. Orleans Territory is established. Napoleon crowns himself emperor of France.

1805—Thomas Jefferson begins his second term as president. Lewis and Clark expedition reaches the Pacific Ocean.

1806—Coinage of silver dollars is stopped; resumes in 1836.

1807—Aaron Burr is acquitted in treason trial. Embargo Act closes U.S. ports to trade.

1808—James Madison is elected president. Congress outlaws importing slaves from Africa.

1810—U.S. population is 7,240,000.

1811—General William Henry Harrison defeats Indians at Tippecanoe. James Monroe is named secretary of state.

1812—Louisiana becomes a state. U.S. declares war on Britain (War of 1812). James Madison is reelected president. Napoleon invades Russia.

1813—British forces take Fort Niagara and Buffalo, New York.

1814—Francis Scott Key writes "The Star-Spangled Banner." British troops burn much of Washington, D.C., including the White House. Treaty of Ghent ends War of 1812. James Monroe becomes secretary of war.

1815—Napoleon meets his final defeat at Battle of Waterloo.

1816—James Monroe is elected president. Indiana becomes a state.

1817—Mississippi becomes a state. Construction on Erie Canal begins.

1818—Illinois enters the Union. The present thirteen-stripe flag is adopted. Border between U.S. and Canada is agreed upon.

1819—Alabama becomes a state. U.S. purchases Florida from Spain. Thomas Jefferson establishes the University of Virginia.

1820—James Monroe is reelected. In the Missouri Compromise, Maine enters the Union as a free (non-slave) state.

1821—Missouri enters the Union as a slave state. Santa Fe Trail opens the American Southwest. Mexico declares independence from Spain. Napoleon Bonaparte dies.

1822—U.S. recognizes Mexico and Colombia. Liberia in Africa is founded as a home for freed slaves.

1823—Monroe Doctrine closes North and South America to colonizing or invasion by European powers.

1824—House of Representatives elects John Quincy Adams president when none of the four candidates wins a majority in national election. Mexico becomes a republic.

1825—Erie Canal is opened. U.S. population is 11,300,000.

1826—Thomas Jefferson and John Adams both die on July 4, the fiftieth anniversary of the Declaration of Independence.

1828—Andrew Jackson is elected president. Tariff of Abominations is passed by Congress, cutting imports.

1829—James Madison attends Virginia's constitutional convention. Slavery is abolished in Mexico.

1830—Indian Removal Act to resettle Indians west of the Mississippi is approved.

1831—James Monroe dies in New York City. Cyrus McCormick develops his reaper.

1832—Andrew Jackson, nominated by the new Democratic Party, is reelected president.

1833—Britain abolishes slavery in its colonies.

1835—Federal government becomes debt-free for the first time.

1836—Martin Van Buren becomes president. Texas wins independence from Mexico. Arkansas joins the Union. James Madison dies at Montpelier, Virginia.

1837—Michigan enters the Union. U.S. population is 15,900,000.

1840—William Henry Harrison is elected president.

1841—President Harrison dies one month after inauguration. Vice-President John Tyler succeeds him.

1844—James Knox Polk is elected president. Samuel Morse sends first telegraphic message.

1845—Texas and Florida become states. Potato famine in Ireland causes massive emigration from Ireland to U.S.

1846—Iowa enters the Union. War with Mexico begins.

1847—U.S. captures Mexico City.

1848—Zachary Taylor becomes president. Treaty of Guadalupe Hidalgo ends Mexico-U.S. war. Wisconsin becomes a state.

1850—President Taylor dies and Vice-President Millard Fillmore succeeds him. California enters the Union, breaking tie between slave and free states.

1852—Franklin Pierce is elected president.

1853—Gadsen Purchase transfers Mexican territory to U.S.

1854—"War for Bleeding Kansas" is fought between slave and free states.

1855—Czar Nicholas I of Russia dies, succeeded by Alexander II.

1856—James Buchanan is elected president. In Massacre of Potawatomie Creek, Kansas-slavers are murdered by free-staters.

1858—Minnesota enters the Union.

1859—Oregon becomes a state.

1860—Abraham Lincoln is elected president; South Carolina secedes from the Union in protest.

1861—Arkansas, Tennessee, North Carolina, and Virginia secede. Kansas enters the Union as a free state. Civil War begins.

1862—Union forces capture Fort Henry, Roanoke Island, Fort Donelson, Jacksonville, and New Orleans; Union armies are defeated at the Battles of Bull Run and Fredricksburg.

1863—Lincoln issues Emancipation Proclamation: all slaves held in rebelling territories are declared free. West Virginia becomes a state.

1864—Abraham Lincoln is reelected. Nevada becomes a state.

1865—Lincoln is assassinated, succeeded by Andrew Johnson. U.S. Civil War ends on May 26. Thirteenth Amendment abolishes slavery.

1867—Nebraska becomes a state. U.S. buys Alaska from Russia for $7,200,000. Reconstruction Acts are passed.

1868—President Johnson is impeached for violating Tenure of Office Act, but is acquitted by Senate. Ulysses S. Grant is elected president. Fourteenth Amendment prohibits voting discrimination.

1870—Fifteenth Amendment gives blacks the right to vote.

1872—Grant is reelected over Horace Greeley. General Amnesty Act pardons ex-Confederates.

1876—Colorado enters the Union. "Custer's last stand": he and his men are massacred by Sioux Indians at Little Big Horn, Montana.

1877—Rutherford B. Hayes is elected president as all disputed votes are awarded to him.

1880—James A. Garfield is elected president.

1881—President Garfield is shot and killed, succeeded by Vice-President Chester A. Arthur.

1882—U.S. bans Chinese immigration for ten years.

1884—Grover Cleveland becomes president.

1886—Statue of Liberty is dedicated.

1888—Benjamin Harrison is elected president.

1889—North Dakota, South Dakota, Washington, and Montana become states.

1890—Idaho and Wyoming become states.

1892—Grover Cleveland is elected president.

1896—William McKinley is elected president. Utah becomes a state.

1898—U.S. declares war on Spain over Cuba.

1899—Philippines demand independence from U.S.

1900—McKinley is reelected. Boxer Rebellion against foreigners in China begins.

1901—McKinley is assassinated by anarchist; he is succeeded by Theodore Roosevelt.

1902—U.S. acquires perpetual control over Panama Canal.

1903—Alaskan frontier is settled.

1904—Russian-Japanese War breaks out. Theodore Roosevelt wins presidential election.

1905—Treaty of Portsmouth signed, ending Russian-Japanese War.

1906—U.S. troops occupy Cuba.

1907—President Roosevelt bars all Japanese immigration. Oklahoma enters the Union.

1908—William Howard Taft becomes president.

1909—NAACP is founded under W.E.B. DuBois

1910—China abolishes slavery.

1911—Chinese Revolution begins.

1912—Woodrow Wilson is elected president. Arizona and New Mexico become states.

1913—Federal income tax is introduced in U.S. through the Sixteenth Amendment.

1914—World War I begins.

1915—British liner *Lusitania* is sunk by German submarine.

1916—Wilson is reelected president.

1917—U.S. breaks diplomatic relations with Germany. Czar Nicholas of Russia abdicates as revolution begins. U.S. declares war on Austria-Hungary.

1918—Wilson proclaims "Fourteen Points" as war aims. On November 11, armistice is signed between Allies and Germany.

1919—Eighteenth Amendment prohibits sale and manufacture of intoxicating liquors. Wilson presides over first League of Nations; wins Nobel Peace Prize.

1920—Nineteenth Amendment (women's suffrage) is passed. Warren Harding is elected president.

1921—Adolf Hitler's stormtroopers begin to terrorize political opponents.

1922—Irish Free State is established. Soviet states form U.S.S.R. Benito Mussolini forms Fascist government in Italy.

1923—President Harding dies; he is succeeded by Vice-President Calvin Coolidge.

1924—Coolidge is elected president.

1925—Hitler reorganizes Nazi Party and publishes first volume of *Mein Kampf.*

1926—Fascist youth organizations founded in Germany and Italy. Republic of Lebanon proclaimed.

1927—Stalin becomes Soviet dictator. Economic conference in Geneva attended by fifty-two nations.

1928—Herbert Hoover is elected president. U.S. and many other nations sign Kellogg-Briand pacts to outlaw war.

1929—Stock prices in New York crash on "Black Thursday"; the Great Depression begins.

1930—Bank of U.S. and its many branches close (most significant bank failure of the year).

1931—Emigration from U.S. exceeds immigration for first time as Depression deepens.

1932—Franklin D. Roosevelt wins presidential election in a Democratic landslide.

1933—First concentration camps are erected in Germany. U.S. recognizes U.S.S.R. and resumes trade. Twenty-First Amendment repeals prohibition.

1934—Severe dust storms hit Plains states. President Roosevelt passes U.S. Social Security Act.

1936—Roosevelt is reelected. Spanish Civil War begins. Hitler and Mussolini form Rome-Berlin Axis.

1937—Roosevelt signs Neutrality Act.

1938—Roosevelt sends appeal to Hitler and Mussolini to settle European problems amicably.

1939—Germany takes over Czechoslovakia and invades Poland, starting World War II.

1940—Roosevelt is reelected for a third term.

1941—Japan bombs Pearl Harbor, U.S. declares war on Japan. Germany and Italy declare war on U.S.; U.S. then declares war on them.

1942—Allies agree not to make separate peace treaties with the enemies. U.S. government transfers more than 100,000 Nisei (Japanese-Americans) from west coast to inland concentration camps.

1943—Allied bombings of Germany begin.

1944—Roosevelt is reelected for a fourth term. Allied forces invade Normandy on D-Day.

1945—President Roosevelt dies; he is succeeded by Harry S Truman. Mussolini is killed; Hitler commits suicide. Germany surrenders. U.S. drops atomic bomb on Hiroshima; Japan surrenders: end of World War II.

1946—U.N. General Assembly holds its first session in London. Peace conference of twenty-one nations is held in Paris.

1947—Peace treaties are signed in Paris. "Cold War" is in full swing.

1948—U.S. passes Marshall Plan Act, providing $17 billion in aid for Europe. U.S. recognizes new nation of Israel. India and Pakistan become free of British rule. Truman is elected president.

1949—Republic of Eire is proclaimed in Dublin. Russia blocks land route access from Western Germany to Berlin; airlift begins. U.S., France, and Britain agree to merge their zones of occupation in West Germany. Apartheid program begins in South Africa.

1950—Riots in Johannesburg, South Africa, against apartheid. North Korea invades South Korea. U.N. forces land in South Korea and recapture Seoul.

1951—Twenty-Second Amendment limits president to two terms.

1952—Dwight D. Eisenhower resigns as supreme commander in Europe and is elected president.

1953—Stalin dies; struggle for power in Russia follows. The Rosenbergs, first sentenced as spies in 1951, are executed.

1954—U.S.-Japan defense agreement signs pact with Nationalist China.

1955—Blacks in Montgomery, Alabama, boycott segregated bus lines.

1956—Eisenhower is reelected president. Soviet troops march into Hungary.

1957—U.S. agrees to withdraw ground forces from Japan. Russia launches first satellite, *Sputnik.*

1958—European Common Market comes into being. Alaska becomes the forty-ninth state. Fidel Castro begins war against Batista government in Cuba.

1959—Hawaii becomes fiftieth state. Castro becomes premier of Cuba. De Gaulle is proclaimed President of the Fifth Republic of France.

1960—Historic debates between Senator John F. Kennedy and Vice-President Richard Nixon are televised. Kennedy is elected president. Brezhnev becomes president of U.S.S.R.

1961—Berlin Wall is constructed. Kennedy and Khrushchev confer in Vienna. In Bay of Pigs incident, Cubans trained by CIA attempt to overthrow Castro.

1962—U.S. military council is established in South Vietnam.

1963—Riots and beatings by police and whites mark civil rights demonstrations in Birmingham, Alabama; 30,000 troops are called out, Martin Luther King, Jr., is arrested. Freedom marchers descend on Washington, D.C., to demonstrate. President Kennedy is assassinated; Vice-President Lyndon B. Johnson is sworn in as president.

1964—U.S. aircraft bomb North Vietnam. Johnson is elected president.

1965—U.S. combat troops arrive in South Vietnam.

1966—International Days of Protest against U.S. policy in Vietnam. National Guard quells race riots in Chicago.

1967—Six-Day War between Israel and Arab nations.

1968—Martin Luther King, Jr., is assassinated in Memphis, Tennessee. Senator Robert Kennedy is assassinated in Los Angeles. Riots and police brutality take place at Democratic National Convention in Chicago. Richard Nixon is elected president. Czechoslovakia is invaded by Soviet and Warsaw Pact troops.

1969—Hundreds of thousands of people in several U.S. cities demonstrate against Vietnam War.

1970—Four Vietnam War protesters are killed by National Guardsmen at Kent State University in Ohio.

1971—Twenty-Sixth Amendment allows eighteen-year-olds to vote.

1972—Nixon visits Communist China; is reelected president in near-record landslide. Watergate affair begins when five men are arrested in the Watergate hotel complex in Washington, D.C. Nixon announces resignations of aides Haldeman, Ehrlichman, and Dean and Attorney General Kleindienst as a result of Watergate-related charges.

1973—Vice-President Spiro Agnew resigns; Gerald Ford is named vice-president. Vietnam peace treaty is formally approved after nineteen months of negotiations.

1974—As a result of Watergate cover-up, impeachment is considered; Nixon resigns and Ford becomes president. Ford pardons Nixon and grants limited amnesty to Vietnam War draft evaders and military deserters.

1975—U.S. civilians are evacuated from Saigon, South Vietnam, as Communist forces complete takeover of South Vietnam.

1976—U.S. celebrates its Bicentennial. James Earl Carter becomes president.

1977—Carter pardons most Vietnam draft evaders, numbering some 10,000.

1980—Ronald Reagan is elected president.

1981—President Reagan is shot in the chest in assassination attempt. Sandra Day O'Connor is appointed first woman justice of the Supreme Court.

1983—U.S. troops invade island of Grenada.

1984—Reagan is reelected president. Democratic candidate Walter Mondale's running mate, Geraldine Ferraro, is the first woman selected for vice-president by a major U.S. political party.

1985—Soviet Communist Party secretary Konstantin Chernenko dies; Mikhail Gorbachev succeeds him. U.S. and Soviet officials discuss arms control in Geneva. Reagan and Gorbachev hold summit conference in Geneva. Racial tensions accelerate in South Africa.

1986—Space shuttle *Challenger* crashes shortly after takeoff; crew of seven dies. U.S. bombs bases in Libya. Corazon Aquino defeats Ferdinand Marcos in Philippine presidential election.

Index

Page numbers in boldface type indicate illustrations.

About the Author

Jim Hargrove has worked as a writer and editor for more than ten years. After serving as an editorial director for three Chicago area publishers, he began a career as an independent writer, preparing a series of books for children. He has contributed to works by nearly twenty different publishers. His Childrens Press titles include biographies of Mark Twain and Richard Nixon. With his wife and daughter, he lives in a small Illinois town near the Wisconsin border.